Poachers

NEL YOMTOV

Children's Press®
An Imprint of Scholastic Inc.

Content Consultant
Albert E. Scherr, JD
Chair, International Criminal Law and Justice Programs
University of New Hampshire School of Law
Concord, New Hampshire

Library of Congress Cataloging-in-Publication Data
Yomtov, Nelson, author.
Poachers / by Nel Yomtov.
   pages cm. — (A true book)
 Summary: "Learn about the illegal hunting of protected animal species, from what methods
poachers use to how governments and other organizations are fighting to end poaching." —
Provided by publisher.
 Includes bibliographical references and index.
 ISBN 978-0-531-21467-1 (library binding) — ISBN 978-0-531-22080-1 (pbk.)
1. Endangered species—Juvenile literature. 2. Poaching—Juvenile literature. 3. Wildlife conserva-
tion—Juvenile literature. I. Title. II. Series: True book.
 QH75.Y66 2016
 333.95'22—dc23   2015023031

**Front cover: Guards stand watch over
an endangered white rhinoceros**
Back cover: Tiger skins poached in China

Find the Truth!

Everything you are about to read is true *except* for one of the sentences on this page.

Which one is **TRUE**?

T or F Poaching is a crime that occurs only in the Southern Hemisphere.

T or F Wildlife crimes affect both animals and humans.

Find the answers in this book.

Contents

THE BIG TRUTH!

Cecil the Lion

Cecil the lion

Hunting has reduced the sitatunga population in Africa.

5 Combating Poaching

What is being done to fight wildlife crime? **37**

Special organizations care for animals whose parents were killed or captured by poachers.

CHAPTER 1

Wildlife Crime

Elephants. Rhinos. Sea turtles. Pythons. Gorillas. Bengal and Siberian tigers. Pangolins. These creatures are all making front-page news lately. It is for bad reasons, however. Each of these **species** is being illegally hunted to near-**extinction** by criminals called **poachers**. Preventing this cruel and often violent crime is a tricky challenge. Sometimes it seems like poachers defeat every attempt to protect Earth's **endangered** animals.

Authorities documented 23 tiger deaths due to poaching in 2014 in India.

The Crime of Poaching

Poaching is the illegal hunting, killing, or removing of any wildlife from its natural **habitat**. This includes mammals, fish, insects, reptiles, and plants. Poaching happens all over the world. It occurs from the plains of Africa and Asia to the rain forests of South and Central America. It even happens in U.S. national parks. Poachers break the laws governments have created to protect wildlife.

A sign urges visitors to report any poaching activity in a protected area in the United States.

People sometimes display tiger skins as trophies.

What Laws Do Poachers Break?

Some laws spell out which species may be hunted and how many of each species a hunter may take. Other laws define the places where hunting is allowed and the time of year it is permitted. Poachers can also violate laws by not having a license or by using certain kinds of weapons or traps. Illegally selling animals or animal parts—such as tusks, claws, or skins—is another serious crime committed by poachers.

Parrots are poached to be sold as pets and for their brightly colored feathers.

What Is Poached?

Poachers set their sights on many kinds of wildlife. Hundreds of species of mammals are poached, including bears, elephants, rhinos, and monkeys. Bird species include eagles, parrots, and owls. Snakes and iguanas are commonly poached reptiles. Sea creatures such as trout, salmon, and shellfish are frequently poached as well. Poachers also prize certain species of cacti, wildflowers, and trees.

Nothing New

Poaching is not new. During the 14th and 15th centuries, a small part of the population owned all the land in Europe. Only these landowners had the right to hunt. To get food, poor people often had to poach animals on a landowner's property. If caught, the people were often hanged. Today's laws are meant to protect wildlife rather than landowners. Poaching is still considered a serious crime, however.

European landowners valued their hunting lands as a source of wealth and amusement.

Russian poachers place an endangered Siberian tiger into a bag.

CHAPTER 2

Who, Why, and How

Poachers are a **diverse** group of people. They may be men or women. They can be young or old. They may hunt alone or with groups. They may be poor or very wealthy, and of any religion or nationality. Some poachers hunt close to home, while others travel to far-off lands. The reasons for poaching are as different as the poachers themselves.

The Soviet Union (now Russia) banned tiger hunting in 1947. Though now illegal, the practice continues.

A Profitable Trade

The main reason for poaching today is money. Poaching is a well-organized, profitable international business. Some poachers sell live animals to collectors of **exotic** species. Others sell animal parts such as bones, furs, and horns on the **black market**. This can earn them large sums of money. Ivory, which comes from elephant tusks, is often carved into jewelry, eating utensils, and other items. It can sell for as much as $1,000 per pound on the streets of China.

Police in New York and Pennsylvania collected several pieces of illegally trafficked ivory figures.

Sharks are fierce hunters, but they can also fall victim to poachers.

Poaching a Meal

Another reason people poach is for food. Some people might hunt and kill wildlife for food when meat is too expensive to purchase or not available. Other people poach because they want to eat a rare **delicacy**. For example, many people in Asia enjoy shark fin soup. To provide the main ingredient, poachers catch sharks, cut off their fins, and toss the sharks back into the water. The injured sharks drown or are eaten by other fish.

A market in Xian, China, sells a wide range of traditional medicines.

Traditional Medicine

In many places, certain animals and plants have value as medicine. For example, in Cambodia, the horn of the water buffalo is used to treat illnesses. In some parts of China, alligator meat is believed to prevent cancer. In many regions, tiger skins, bones, teeth, and claws are used in traditional medicine to cure toothaches and even to shield people from curses.

Trophy Poaching

There are also people who poach for fun or for trophies. Big-game hunters often hunt for animals with the biggest manes, antlers, tusks, or horns. In 2014, U.S. authorities fined two men from South Africa for guiding American hunters on illegal big-game hunts. The hunters paid between $3,500 and $15,000 to hunt rhinoceroses. After the hunters shot the rhinos, the two guides cut off the horns and sold them on the black market.

Overhunting animals such as Africa's sitatunga, a type of antelope, is causing species' populations to decrease rapidly.

Methods of Poachers

Poachers use a variety of methods to trap animals. One example is snare wires, which are cables tied onto trees. The snare is positioned to trap an animal by the neck or legs. The more the animal struggles to free itself, the more the snare tightens. Poachers in Africa use snare wires to trap antelopes and other forest animals for meat. Often, other animals such as gorillas, cheetahs, and giraffes accidentally get caught in the snares and die.

A member of an antipoaching patrol holds up a snare trap found in Volcanoes National Park in Rwanda.

It is illegal to hunt alligators in much of the United States, though restaurants and grocery stores can legally sell meat that comes from alligator farms.

Markets and Restaurants

For hunters and traders in some regions, hunting animals is an important part of their culture or religion. For these reasons, illegal wildlife markets and restaurants thrive in these locations. In the town of Mong La in Myanmar, along the border with China, outdoor shops sell elephant hides and tusks, leopard and bear skins, antelope skulls, and other items. Sun bear meat and monkey meat are common dishes served in restaurants there.

Hunters most often use rifles, and occasionally bows, when hunting elk.

Extreme Poaching

Many poachers use poison to capture or kill animals. For example, poachers in the Congo put poison on their arrow tips. Some poachers use machine guns and explosives to kill. Others may hunt from an airplane or land vehicle by shooting at fleeing animals. Many countries have laws that ban these practices. Poaching is difficult to stop, and poachers are difficult to track.

Meet a Poacher

John Kaimoi Sumokwo was once a poacher in Kenya. He admitted to killing 70 elephants for their tusks and served two years in jail for his crime. Before he began poaching, he planted corn to earn a living. When a drought ruined his crops, he began hunting elephants to earn money. Sumokwo says that killing made him feel "inhuman" and guilty. But he had to continue doing it to feed his family. Today, Sumokwo no longer poaches. He believes people must be taught how important wild animals are to the environment.

The skulls of poached elephants and rhinoceroses are displayed at South Luangwa National Park in Zambia.

CHAPTER 3

The Impact of Wildlife Poaching

Poaching has a harmful impact on wildlife populations, the environment, and human communities. It threatens the extinction of certain species and causes pain and suffering to animals. It also damages natural habitats. This in turn can destroy delicate **ecosystems** that other wildlife depend on. Poaching also encourages other kinds of crime and endangers human health.

Elephants and rhinoceroses are poached for the ivory of their tusks and horns.

Grevy's zebras are at risk of disappearing forever because of extensive poaching.

Effects on Wildlife Populations

Poaching is the greatest threat to many animal species. In parts of Asia, bear organs and paws are used to make traditional medicines. This has caused huge population declines in six of the world's eight bear species. In East Africa, the population of Grevy's zebra has dropped from 25,000 to 2,500 over the past 40 years because poachers kill the animals for their skins.

Effect on the Environment

Poaching also affects the animals that aren't directly hunted. For example, baby elephants are often left to survive on their own when adults are killed for their tusks and hides. In addition, poachers who remove animals or plants from their ecosystems upset the balance of food that is available in an area. If deer-hunting wolves are poached, for example, the deer population may become too large.

Then there won't be enough plants to feed all the deer.

A baby elephant, orphaned due to poaching, wears a custom-made raincoat at The David Sheldrick Wildlife Trust in Kenya.

Park wardens in Chobe National Park in Bostwana display elephant tusks taken from poachers.

Rise in Crime

Poaching has an impact on humans, too. Law enforcement officers, poachers, and innocent people often die because of poaching. From 2003 to 2013, poachers killed at least 1,000 forest rangers in 35 countries. In some places in India and Africa, forest guards have the legal authority to shoot poachers on sight. In Kenya, poachers have killed tourists who stumbled upon the hunters' illegal activities. Poaching has been linked to organized crime groups and even the illegal drug trade.

A Threat to Public Health

Outbreaks of deadly diseases are also sometimes connected to poaching. In Africa, the spread of Ebola has been traced to people eating poached meat, possibly from bats. In Hong Kong, severe acute respiratory syndrome (SARS) has been linked to human contact with poached meat from **primates**. Bird flu can be passed to humans who eat illegally traded chickens and ducks that have gotten the disease from wild birds.

Consuming meat from some wild animals can result in the spread of deadly diseases.

Parrots and other exotic birds are often packed together in tight spaces as they are transported out of their home countries.

CHAPTER 4

A Global Threat

The global demand for exotic wildlife is enormous. The World Wildlife Fund (WWF) is an organization that works to protect endangered wildlife. It reports that more than 110 million tons of fish, 1.5 million live birds, and 440,000 tons of plants are sold or traded in just one year. The more people are willing to pay for these plants and animals, the more poachers are encouraged to hunt.

Large numbers of parrots are poached deep within the forests of Central America.

North America

Hundreds of wildlife species are poached each year in North America. Poachers kill elk, moose, and bighorn sheep to take their heads and antlers as trophies. Walruses are poached for their ivory tusks, and bald eagles are captured for their feathers. Millions of plants, including rare orchids and trees, are illegally collected. In Mexico, river otters are killed for their fur and parrots are trapped for the pet trade.

Elk hunting is strictly controlled in the United States. Elk hunters must follow certain rules, such as having a special permit and hunting only at certain times of the year.

Wild animals experience a great deal of stress when placed in captivity.

Central and South America

The lush rain forests and warm coastal waters of Central and South America are prime hunting grounds for poachers. Dozens of species of rare, colorful birds are poached for their feathers and beaks. Iguanas, monkeys, ocelots, snakes, turtles, and tortoises are captured and sold as pets. Large numbers of West Indian manatees are poached for their meat. Their bones are carved into trinkets and tourist souvenirs.

Africa

Elephants and rhinos are the main targets of poachers in Africa. Elephants are poached for their ivory tusks. The number of African elephants has dropped more than 70 percent since the early 1980s. By 2013, an estimated 419,000 remained, down from 26 million in the early 1700s. The horns of the white and black rhinoceroses are used for traditional medicine, mainly in Asia. Since 1960, the black rhino population in Africa has decreased almost 98 percent.

Timeline of Poaching History

1700
Poaching laws are enacted in Europe for the first time.

1947
The Soviet Union bans tiger hunting after fewer than 40 Siberian tigers are found living in the wild.

Asia

Elephants and rhinos are also poached in Asia. So are many other species. For example, male Siberian musk deer are killed for their scent glands. These organs are used to make perfumes and medicines. Pangolins are highly prized for their scales, which are used in medicine. Their meat is a luxury food in China. The Gold of Kinabulu orchid and Thailand rosewood timber are Asian plant species that have been poached close to extinction.

1989

An international ban on the ivory trade goes into effect to reduce elephant poaching.

2010–2012

Poachers kill more than 100,000 African elephants. This equals about 20 percent of the continent's elephant population.

Cecil the Lion

In Hwange National Park in Zimbabwe, visitors flocked to visit Cecil the lion. Cecil was easy to recognize with his long black mane. But in July 2015, Cecil's fans around the world had a shock. The lion had been lured out of the park and killed after a 40-hour hunt. The hunter was Walter Palmer, a dentist from Minnesota.

Public Response

News of Cecil's death spread fast. People were sad and angry. Some posted messages on Web sites such as Facebook in protest. Others left signs, stuffed animals, and other objects at Palmer's homes and at his dental office.

Government Response

Before, Zimbabwe had allowed limited hunting of lions and other animals. After Cecil's death, however, the government suspended all lion, elephant, and leopard hunting. Officials arrested two Zimbabwe residents involved in the hunt, including Palmer's hunting guide (pictured). They also asked the U.S. government to send Palmer to Zimbabwe for a trial.

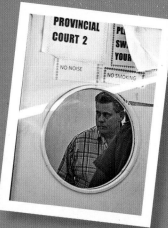

In the United States, lawmakers started work on the Conserving Ecosystems by Ceasing the Importation of Large (CECIL) Animal Trophies Act. If passed, this new law would ban bringing endangered animal hunting trophies into the country.

A black rhinoceros hangs from a helicopter as officials move the animal to a nature reserve where it will be protected.

CHAPTER 5

Combating Poaching

Poaching is unlikely to ever be stopped completely. It is an international issue, and it is very difficult to keep track of. Even as one government enacts new laws, another may turn a blind eye to the illegal trade of wildlife. Poachers around the world will likely continue committing crimes against wildlife and damaging the environment. Fortunately, there are many people working to keep the situation from getting worse.

Helicopters help people to move large animals safely and quickly.

Officials in Kenya burn more than 20 tons of elephant tusks taken from poachers to keep the ivory from being sold.

Major Organizations

Many groups work to protect wildlife and educate the public about poaching. The WWF works with governments to establish antipoaching regulations. The Sea Shepherd Conservation Society in Washington investigates poaching of marine life such as whales, fish, and seabirds. New York City's Wildlife Conservation Society and the African Wildlife Foundation, based in Kenya, work to protect species around the world.

Antipoaching Rangers

Many governments train armed rangers to patrol areas where poachers are likely to operate. These wildlife rangers face many of the same dangers as soldiers in wartime. Many poachers are willing to hurt anyone who stands in their way. The Southern African Wildlife College is a school that trains rangers in observational skills, tracking techniques, and shooting ability. The school also offers courses in **stealth** techniques for observing and capturing poachers at work.

Armed guards protect one of the last remaining wild northern white rhinoceroses from poachers.

A High-Tech Battle

Rangers use a variety of high-tech devices against poachers. Unmanned aerial vehicles (UAVs), or drones, are equipped with cameras and flown over areas where poachers are known to strike. Armed with the information sent back by the UAV, rangers are able to move in on the poachers by foot or helicopter. Because most poachers work in the darkness, rangers use night-vision goggles. They also use satellite imagery to monitor poaching locations and develop flight plans for UAVs.

A wildlife official at Kaziranga National Park in India prepares to test a new drone.

Defending Animals

Damien Mander is a former military sniper who served in the Australian Royal Navy. After fighting in the Iraq War, Mander traveled throughout Africa. There, he witnessed the effects of poaching firsthand. Mander decided to use his military skills to help prevent poaching. In 2009, he formed the International Anti-Poaching Foundation (IAPF). The IAPF teaches rangers how to conduct raids and plan antipoaching patrols. It operates in South Africa, Australia, Zimbabwe, and Mozambique.

What You Can Do

Poaching is a global crime. Its effects are felt all around the world by people, plants, and animals alike. It is a serious problem that threatens the environment and the species that live in it. It might seem like something that only trained professionals can deal with. All people can help prevent poaching, however, by being mindful of the ways the illegal trade of animals and plants can spread from country to country.

Exotic animals such as lizards might seem like good pets, but they are not meant to live outside of their natural habitats.

Fighting poaching also helps protect natural areas such as the Amazon rain forest.

One important step is to avoid buying products that come from poaching. Don't buy exotic animals from pet shops or dealers. Instead, adopt a domestic animal from a shelter or rescue group. Don't buy animal products if you travel to foreign countries. Urge the adults around you to sign petitions to protect wildlife. Better yet, start your own petitions with your friends and send them to local government officials! ★

True Statistics

Number of rhinoceroses killed in South Africa in 2014: 1,215, or about one every eight hours

Number of African elephants killed by poachers between 2011 and 2012: More than 100,000

Loss of elephant population in central Africa between 2000 and 2015: 64 percent

Amount of illegal ivory seized in China in a single incident, 2013: 12 tons, worth more than $9.5 million

Decrease in India's Bengal tiger population: From 3,600 in the late 1990s to 1,700 in 2015

Prices of poached items in China: A single tiger skin, $20,000; a large rhino horn, $37,000

Number of people arrested for rhino poaching in South Africa in 2013: 343

Did you find the truth?

(F) Poaching is a crime that occurs only in the southern hemisphere.

(T) Wildlife crimes affect both animals and humans.

Resources

Books

Baillie, Marilyn. *How to Save a Species*. Berkeley, CA: Owlkids, 2014.

Blewett, Ashlee Brown. *Mission: Elephant Rescue: All About Elephants and How to Save Them*. Washington, DC: National Geographic Society, 2014.

Hibbert, Clare. *Orangutan Orphans*. New York: PowerKids Press, 2015.

Hirsch, Rebecca. *Helping Endangered Animals*. Ann Arbor, MI: Cherry Lake Publishing, 2010.

Visit this Scholastic Web site for more information on poachers:
★ www.factsfornow.scholastic.com
Enter the keyword **Poachers**

Important Words

black market (BLACK MAHR-kit) the trade of buying or selling illegal goods

delicacy (DEL-ih-kuh-see) something pleasing to eat that is considered rare

diverse (dye-VURS) having many different types or kinds

ecosystems (EE-koh-sis-tuhmz) all the living things in places and their relationship to their environment

endangered (en-DAYN-jurd) at risk of dying out completely

exotic (ig-ZAH-tik) from a faraway country

extinction (ik-STINGKT-shun) the state or process of a species dying out completely

habitat (HAB-uh-tat) the place where an animal or plant is usually found

poachers (POH-churz) people who hunt, fish, or gather plants illegally

primates (PRYE-mates) any members of the group of mammals that includes monkeys, apes, and humans

species (SPEE-sheez) one of the groups into which animals and plants of the same genus are divided

stealth (STELTH) silent, secret, and careful movement

Index

Page numbers in **bold** indicate illustrations.

About the Author

Nel Yomtov is an award-winning author with a passion for writing nonfiction books for young readers. He has written books and graphic novels about history, geography, science, and other subjects.

Nel has worked at Marvel Comics, where he edited, wrote, and colored hundreds of titles. He has also served as editorial director of a children's book publisher and as publisher of Hammond World Atlas books.

Yomtov lives in the New York City area with his wife, Nancy, a teacher. Their son, Jess, is a sports journalist.